The month of December, from the illuminated manuscript *Les Très Riches Heures du duc de Berry*

The Story of a Special Day
Volume 345

December

10

344th day of the year
(345th in leap years)
21 days remaining
until the end of the year.

by Michael Dobson

Timespinner
Press

This book is also available in e-book form for Kindle, e-pub devices, and other formats from your favorite online booksellers.

For more information about the series, about us, or about your special day, please email us at editor@timespinnerpress.com.

Look for other volumes in *The Story of a Special Day*, coming often. See www.timespinnerpress.com for details and for the most recent information.

Table of Contents

Cover: Edward VIII, Wallis Simpson, and the Instrument of Abdication on a background of the Duke of Windsor's Coat of Arms— for the *Event of the Day.*

Back Cover and Frontispiece: The month of December, from the French Gothic illuminated manuscript *Les Très Riches Heures du duc de Berry.*

December 10
Quotations

My friends are my "estate." Forgive me then the avarice to hoard them.

— *Emily Dickinson, born December 10, 1830*

Laughter is the closest thing to the grace of God.

— *Karl Barth, died December 10, 1968*

I occasionally play works by contemporary composers and for two reasons. First to discourage the composer from writing any more and secondly to remind myself how much I appreciate Beethoven.

— Jascha Heifetz, died December 10, 1987

Glamour is just sex that got civilized.

— *Dorothy Lamour, born December 10, 1914*

Rosa Parks showed us all that one little person can make a whole bunch of noise without so much as a whisper. She showed the world that the color of your skin shouldn't determine what part of the bus you sit in...as you ride through life.

— *Richard Pryor, died December 10, 2005*

The only thing that saves us from the bureaucracy is inefficiency. An efficient bureaucracy is the greatest threat to liberty.

— *Eugene McCarthy, died December 10, 2005*

Event of the Day

The Abdication Crisis

On December 10, 1936, Edward VIII, King of the United Kingdom and Emperor of India, became the only British monarch to voluntarily renounce the throne since the Anglo-Saxon period.

Oldest son of the future King George V and Queen Mary, Edward was born on June 23, 1894. His father became king in 1910 and Edward became Prince of Wales. He attended Oxford and served in both the Royal Navy and the Grenadier Guards, serving in World War I.

After the war, he gained a reputation as a playboy. His father became increasingly disappointed, claiming, "After I am dead, the boy will ruin himself in 12 months."

In 1931, Edward met married American socialite Wallis Simpson. Wallis had been married once previously to a US Navy pilot, but divorced him in 1927. Before that divorce became final, she became involved with British shipping executive Ernest Simpson, who divorced his wife and married Wallis the following year. Over the next few years, the Simpsons and the Prince of Wales met at various parties, and at some point the two became lovers.

In January 1936, King George V died, and Edward VIII ascended to the throne. Wallis attended royal functions as the King's guest. That summer

Wallis and Edward took a long and scandalous Mediterranean cruise in a yacht belonging to the Romanian royal family.

Edward VIII and Wallis Simpson during their Mediterranean vacation

By the fall, it was widely rumored that Edward planned to marry Wallis. She filed for divorce from her second husband, and in November, Edward informed the Prime Minister of his intent, but was told that the marriage would not be acceptable. There were several objections.

First, the King of Great Britain was the nominal head of the Church of England. At that time, the church did not permit divorced people to remarry if their ex-spouses were still alive.

Socially, the previous marriages also made Wallis Simpson unsuitable. It didn't help that many assumed that her motives were financial or status, rather than love for the king.

Foreign policy played a role. There were rumors that Simpson was a Nazi agent who was simultaneously having an affair with German ambassador Joachim von Ribbentrop. There were also tensions with the United States that made an American woman even more unsuitable.

There was some support for the marriage. Some were willing to accept Wallis Simpson as Edward's wife on the condition she was not also made Queen.

The growing constitutional crisis came to a head quickly, and it became increasingly clear that abdication was the only alternative if Edward was unwilling to give up marrying Simpson. He signed the notice of abdication on December 10, witnessed by his three younger brothers. The following day, he made a speech to the nation, which contained the famous line that he would be unable to do his job "as I would have wished" without the support of "the woman I love."

At 327 days, Edward's reign as King was the shortest of any British monarch since Lady Jane Grey, nearly 400 years previously. He was succeeded by his younger brother Albert, Duke of York, who became King George VI. Because the planned coronation of Edward VIII had not yet taken place, the ceremony continued on schedule with the new monarch.

Following the abdication, Edward was given the title of His Royal Highness the Duke of Windsor, and he and Wallis Simpson married the following year. The couple spent most of the rest of their lives in France, though he was appointed Governor of the Bahamas during World War II. There were rumors that he and his wife were Nazi sympathizers who hoped that a Hitler victory would return him to the throne. The couple lived on an allowance from Goerge VI, with additional money from memoirs and illegal currency trading. They had no children.

The Duke of Windsor died on May 28, 1972. The Duchess of Windsor died on April 24, 1986. Both are buried in the Royal Burial Ground near Windsor Castle.

Coat of Arms of the Duke of Windsor

December 10 Holidays and Celebrations

Nobeldagen (Sweden)

Alfred Nobel Day, occasion of the presentation of the Nobel Prize.

Constitution Day (Thailand)

Commemorating Thailand's first permanent constitution in 1932.

Human Rights Day (International)

Honoring the 1950 United Nations adoption of the Universal Declaration of Human Rights.

Christian Feast Days

In **Western Christianity**, December 10 is the feast day of Saint Eulalia of Mérida, Saint Miltiades, and the Translation of the Holy House of Loreto..

In **Eastern Orthodox Christianity**, December 10 is the feast of Menas the Most Eloquent, Gemellus of Paphlagonia, Pope Saint Gregory III, Saint Sindulf of Vienne, and Saint Guitmarus. (These events are observed on December 23 by "Old Calendarists.")

Portrait of Catherine Howard by Hans Holbein the Younger

What Happened on December 10?

1520 — **Martin Luther Defies the Pope**

Martin Luther first challenged the Catholic Church in 1517, with what became known as the Ninety-Five Theses. In 1520, Pope Leo X issued a papal bull, *Exurge Domine*, threatening Martin Luther with excommunication if he did not recant. In response, on December 10, 1520, Martin Luther publicly burned a copy of the bull, which signaled his final break with Catholicism and the beginning of the Protestant Reformation.

1541 — **Execution of Queen Catherine's Lovers**

After his fourth marriage to Anne of Cleves was annulled, King Henry VIII of England married Catherine Howard, who was about 30 years younger, three weeks later. Soon, Queen Catherine began a romance with Thomas Culpepper, who was the king's favorite courtier. When their relationship was exposed, Francis Derham, another courtier who had been involved with Catherine before her marriage to Henry, was caught in the scandal. On December 10, 1541, both men were executed. Catherine survived until February 1542, when she, too, was beheaded.

1817 — **Mississippi Becomes the 20th US State**

On December 10, 1817, the Mississippi Territory, which had been won by the British from the French in 1763 and subsequently incorporated into the newly-formed United States of America, became the 20th state admitted to the Union.

1868 — **First Traffic Lights**

On December 10, 1868, the first traffic lights were installed outside Westminster Palace in London. They had semaphore arms and were illuminated by red and green gas lamps.

1869 — **Kappa Sigma Founded**

Although the Kappa Sigma (KΣ) fraternity claims to derive from a secret society founded in 1400, its first official chapter was founded on December 10, 1869, at the University of Virginia.

1884 — **Huckleberry Finn is Published**

The first edition of Mark Twain's *The Adventures of Huckleberry Finn*, widely considered one of the finest works in American literature, but controversial for its language and treatment of racial matters, was published in Canada and England on December 10, 1884. The first US edition appeared the following February.

Mark Twain's Latest Book.

THE ADVENTURES OF

HUCKLEBERRY FINN.

TOM SAWYER'S COMRADE.

A PIRATE FOR THIRTY YEARS.
(Page 104 Huckleberry Finn.)

Every Line Fresh and New.

NOT a sentence of this book has ever before appeared in print in any form.
All the illustrations are New, and were made expressly for this book at great expense.

WRITTEN IN MARK TWAIN'S OLD STYLE.

This book is simply irresistible, and is pronounced by an author of WORLD-WIDE reputation and HIGH AUTHORITY, who has read the manuscript, "The brightest and most humorous book that Mark Twain has ever written."

A BOOK FOR THE YOUNG AND THE OLD, THE RICH AND THE POOR.

A CURE FOR MELANCHOLY.—Nine-tenths of our ills are due to an over-burdened mind, an over-taxed brain, or imaginary troubles that never come. An amusing book is a panacea more agreeable than medicine and less expensive than doctors' bills.

A MINE OF HUMOR.

Full of startling incidents and hair-breadth escapes, 366 PAGES and 174 ORIGINAL ILLUSTRATIONS, NEARLY ONE HUNDRED PAGES LARGER THAN "ADVENTURES OF TOM SAWYER," with fourteen more illustrations, better printed, and more attractively bound, yet offered at the SAME PRICE. This book also contains a full-paged heliotype of the bust of the author by Karl Gerhardt, with fac-simile autograph.

HARD FACTS!

Five Hundred and Twenty-five Thousand (over Half a Million) Copies of Mark Twain's Books have been sold in this Country alone; to Say nothing of the immense sales in England, Germany and other parts of the world.

MARK TWAIN'S BOOKS ARE THE QUICKEST SELLING IN THE WORLD.

In REVERTING TO HIS OLD STYLE OF WRITING, Mark Twain is certainly in his element; for this book, while INTENSELY interesting as a narrative—holding the reader's attention with a tenacity that admits of no economy in the mid-night oil—is also at the top of the list as a humorous work. Interwoven in its text are side-splitting stories, sly hints at different weaknesses of society, and adventures of the most humorous description.

ALL of its FORTY THREE CHAPTERS are SIMPLY OVERFLOWING WITH INTEREST & HUMOR

In the abstract, the book is the story of adventures of Huckleberry Finn, Tom Sawyer and a negro named Jim, who, in their travels fall in with two tramps engaged in TAKING IN the different country towns through which they pass, by means of the missionary dodge, the temperance crusade, or under any pretext that offers to EASILY raise a dishonest dollar.

The writer follows these characters through their various adventures, until we find the tramps properly and warmly clothed—WITH A COAT OF TAR AND FEATHERS—and the boys and Jim escape their prosecutors and return safely to their friends.

THIS BOOK IS A COMPANION TO "THE ADVENTURES OF TOM SAWYER," but is complete in itself. No possessor of a Mark Twain book should be without this last and best of his works.

Parties wishing "The Adventures of Tom Sawyer," "The Prince and the Pauper," or any other of Mark Twain's books, can procure them of the agent. No MONEY IS REQUIRED UNTIL THE DELIVERY OF THE BOOK, and no obligation rests with any subscriber to take the book unless it equals in every respect the description given in our circular and the sample shown. The book is now ready and a preliminary canvass proves that it will be the most popular and successful of all of Twain's books. The Richest, Wittiest and funniest. One agent reports 60 orders in half a day and 95 in six days. Another, that the "very name" sells the book without further effort than the mere offering of the prospectus for signature. Send for canvassing outfit at once and secure good territory.

SOLD ONLY BY SUBSCRIPTION.

Price in Fine Cloth Binding, Plain Edges,	·	·	·	·	·	**$3.50.**
Leather Library Style, Sprinkled Edges,	·	·	·	·	·	**4.00.**
Half Morocco, Marbled Edges,	·	·	·	·	·	**5.50.**

See the Book.   It Speakes For Itself.

FOR AN AGENCY ADDRESS IMMEDIATELY

THE OCCIDENTAL PUBLISHING COMPANY,

No. 120 Sutter Street,   **San Francisco, Cal.**

Promotional flyer for *The Adventures of Huckleberry Finn,* 1884

1898 — **Spanish-American War Ends**

On December 10, 1898, the Spanish-American War officially ended with the signing of the Treaty of Paris. It was the end of the Spanish Empire in America and the beginning of United States colonial power.

1899 — **Delta Sigma Phi Founded**

Delta Sigma Phi (ΔΣΦ), the first fraternity to contain both Christians and Jews, was founded on December 10, 1899, at the City College of New York.

1901 — **First Nobel Prizes**

In 1888, Alfred Nobel, Swedish arms manufacturer and inventor of dynamite, was shocked to find his own obituary in a French newspaper. It was an error; it was actually Alfred's brother who had died.

But what shocked Alfred Nobel the most was the headline: "The Merchant of Death is Dead." This was not how he wanted to be remembered. As a result of this shock, he changed his will to specify that his fortune would be used to create prizes for those who contributed "the greatest benefit on mankind." The categories were physics, chemistry, peace, physiology or medicine, and literature.

Alfred died on December 10, 1896, and shortly thereafter the Nobel Foundation established the process for awarding the prizes. Beginning in 1901, the Nobel Prizes are awarded on December 10 of each year, interrupted only by World War II.

Alfred Nobel

1904 — **Pi Kappa Phi Founded**

Pi Kappa Phi (ΠΚΦ), a social fraternity that operates
the Push America philanthropy, was founded
December 10, 1904, at the College of Charleston,
South Carolina.

1906 — **First American Wins a Nobel Prize**

On December 10,
1906, US President
Theodore Roosevelt
won the Nobel Peace
Prize, the first
American to be
honored with a Nobel.

Nobel Prize photo of
Theodore Roosevelt, 1906

1911 — **First Transcontinental Flight Completed**

Competing for the Hearst $50,000 prize for the
first aviator to fly from coast to coast across the
United States, Cal Rodgers, flying a customized
Wright EX biplane named the *Vin Fiz* (after a then-
popular soft drink), landed in Long Beach,
California, and taxied his plane into the Pacific
Ocean.

The trip, which began in Sheepshead Bay, New York, on September 17, 1911, took 70 stops to make the trip. Today, the *Vin Fiz* can be seen in the Smithsonian Institution's National Air and Space Museum.

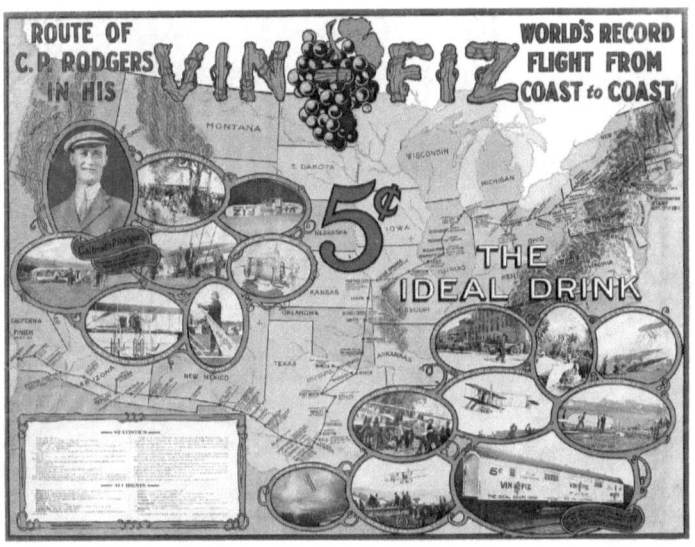

Advertising poster for the *Vin Fiz* transcontinental flight

1935 — **First Heisman Trophy Awarded**

On December 10, 1935, the Downtown Athletic Club awarded a trophy (later renamed the Heisman Trophy) to halfback Jay Berwanger of the University of Chicago.

1955 — *Mighty Mouse Playhouse* Premiers

Mighty Mouse, a cartoon parody of Superman, brought his adventures to TV starting December 10, 1955. The show would run for nearly twelve years. (Fun fact: "Mighty Mouse" was originally conceived as a super-powered housefly named "Superfly.")

Mighty Mouse

1968 — The "300 Million Yen Robbery" Takes Place

On the morning of December 10, 1968, thieves posing as policemen robbed a bank car carrying 300 million yen, or nearly US$4 million. It was the largest robbery in Japanese history, and remains unsolved to this day.

Who Was Born on December 10?

Actors and Other Performers

Raven-Symoné (December 10, 1960 —)

Actress and singer Raven-Symoné began her career on the TV sitcom *The Cosby Show* and later starred in the Disney Channel series *That's So Raven*. A singer as well, she has had several albums go double-platinum.

Kenneth Branagh (December 10, 1960 —)

Kenneth Branagh directed and starred in several film adaptations of Shakespeare plays, receiving Oscar nominations for *Henry V* and *Hamlet*. He appeared in numerous films and TV series, including *Harry Potter and the Chamber of Secrets*.

Susan Dey (December 10, 1952 —)

Actress Susan Dey is best known for her roles in the 1970s sitcom *The Partridge Family* and the 1980s drama *L. A. Law*.

Tommy Kirk (December 10, 1941 —)

Tommy Kirk starred in a number of Disney movies, including *Old Yeller* and *The Shaggy Dog,* and went on to star in various 1960s beach party films including *Pajama Party* and *The Ghost in the Invisible Bikini.*

Dan Blocker (December 10, 1928 — May 13, 1972)

Dan Blocker was best known for his role as "Hoss" in the TV western series *Bonanza.*

Dan Blocker

Harold Gould (December 10, 1923 — September 11, 2010)

Harold Gould appeared in the sitcoms *The Golden Girls* and *Rhoda,* for which he received five Emmy nominations, and appeared in numerous plays and movies, including *The Sting.*

Dorothy Lamour (December 10, 1914 — September 22, 1996)

Dorothy Lamour was a movie star best known for appearing in the *Road to...* movies starring Bing Crosby and Bob Hope. She was a popular pinup girl for American servicemen in World War II.

Dorothy Lamour

Hermes Pan (December 10, 1910 — September 19, 1990)

Dancer and choreographer Hermes Pan was Fred Astaire's collaborator on numerous musicals, including the Astaire and Rogers films. He received an Oscar in 1937 for Best Dance Direction.

Una Merkel (December 10, 1903 — January 2, 1986)

Tony Award-winning stage and film actress Una Merkel (left) began her career in silent movies and went on to a long career as an MGM contract player. Her best-known roles include *Destry Rides Again* with Marlene Dietrich and *The Bank Dick* with W. C. Fields.

Musicians

Nia Peeples (December 10, 1961 —)

Nia Peeples is best known for her role as Nicole Chapman in the TV series *Fame*. Her biggest hit single, "Street of Dreams," was #12 on the Hot 100 in 1991. She was the host of *Top of the Pops* and *The Machine With Nia Peeples,* and appeared on *The Young and the Restless* and *Walker: Texas Ranger.*

Chad Stuart (December 10, 1941 —)

Chad Stuart, half of the British Invasion folk rock duo Chad & Jeremy, had seven US Top 40 hits between 1964 and 1966.

Chad & Jeremy. Chad Stuart (left) and Jeremy Clyde (right), 1966

Alexander Courage (December 10, 1919 — May 5, 2008)

Best known for composing the theme song for the television series *Star Trek,* Courage was also an orchestrator/arranger and composer for numerous movies and television series.

Morton Gould (December 10, 1913 — February 21, 1996)

Morton Gould wrote the score for the Broadway hit *Billion Dollar Baby,* scored a number of TV series and movies, and wrote a number of symphonic works. He received a Pulitzer Prize for Music in 1995 and a Grammy Lifetime Achievement Award in 2005.

Politics and Government

Rod Blagojevich (December 10, 1961 —)

Governor of Illinois from 2003 to 2009, Blagojevich was arrested in 2008 on Federal corruption charges and subsequently impeached and removed from office. He was convicted in 2011 and sentenced to 14 years in prison.

Abu Abbas (ابو عباس) (December 10, 1948 — March 8, 2004)

Syrian militant Abu Abbas founded the Palentine Liberation Front (PLF). He mastermined the hijacking of the Italian cruise ship *Achille Lauro* in 1985. He was captured by American forces in Iraq in 2003, and died in captivity the following year.

Philip Hart (December 10, 1912 — December 26, 1976)

A US senator from Illinois, Hart served in Congress from 1959 until his death in 1976. He was known as "the conscience of the Senate." The Hart Senate Office Building is named for him.

Chet Huntley (December 10, 1911 — March 20, 1974)

Television newscaster Chet Huntley was best known as co-anchor of the NBC evening news program *The Huntley-Brinkley Report.*

Chet Huntley (right) with David Brinkley from
The Huntley-Brinkley Report, 1963

Science and Education

Ada Lovelace (December 10, 1815 — November 27, 1852)

Augusta Ada King, Countess of Lovelace, was the only legitimate child of the poet Lord Byron. A gifted mathematician, she worked on Charles Babbage's mechanical computer, the "analytical engine." She wrote the first algorithm intended to be processed by a machine, earning the title of "the world's first programmer." The computer language Ada is named for her.

Thomas Gallaudet (December 10, 1787 — September 10, 1851)

The Reverend Thomas Gallaudet was an American pioneer in the education of the deaf, and co-founded the first institution for the education of the deaf in North America, the American School for the Deaf. Gallaudet University takes its name from him.

Sports

Matt Forté (December 10, 1985 —)

Matt Forté became a football running back for the Chicago Bears in 2008. He played college football at Tulane University.

Ada Lovelace, by Margaret Sarah Carpenter

JTG (December 10, 1984 —)

Born Jayson Paul, JTG (Just That Gangsta) is a WWE professional wrestler.

Mr. Águila (December 10, 1978 —)

José Seldano is a Mexican professional wrestler (*luchador*) who has worked both in Mexico and in the US.

Bryant Stith (December 10, 1970 —)

Retired NBA shooting guard Bryant Stith played for the Denver Nuggets, Boston Celtics, and the Cleveland Cavaliers, and played for the US national team in the 1990 FIBA World Championship, winning the bronze medal.

Mark Aguirre (December 10, 1959 —)

Retired NBA player Mark Aguirre won two championships with the Detroit Pistons, and was a three-time all-star for the Dallas Mavericks.

Steve Renko (December 10, 1944 —)

Former MLB player Steve Renko played for the Montreal Expos, Chicago Cubs and White Sox, Oakland As, Boston Red Sox, and other teams. He is 99th on the career home runs list.

Words

Melvil Dewey (December 10, 1851 — December 26, 1931)

Librarian Melvil Dewey invented the Dewey Decimal system of library classification, still used in over 200,000 libraries in at least 135 countries.

Emily Dickinson (December 10, 1830 — May 15, 1886)

Emily Dickinson is a major American poet. Although few of her poems were published in her lifetime, after her death several collections of her poetry were published, and have gained increasing critical respect over the years.

Emily Dickinson

George MacDonald (December 10, 1824 — September 18, 1905)

Scottish author and minister George Macdonald is primarily known for his fairy tales and fantasy novels, which inspired authors including W. H. Auden, J. R. R. Tolkien, C. S. Lewis, and Madeline L'Engle. His most famous work is *The Princess and the Goblin.*

George MacDonald (Photo: Lewis Carroll)

Who Died on December 10?

Actors and Other Performers

Richard Pryor (December 1, 1940 — December 10, 2005)

Actor, comedian, social critic, and author Richard Pryor (right) was widely considered one of the most influential stand-up comics of his era, praised by Jerry Seinfeld (who called him "the Picasso of our profession"), Bob Newhart, Bill Cosby, and others. He won an Emmy, five Grammy Awards, and was the first winner of the Kennedy Center Mark Twain Prize for American Humor.

Shirley Hemphill (July 1, 1947 — December 10, 1999)

Stand-up comedienne and actress Shirley Hemphill is best known for her role on the 1970s sitcom *What's Happening!!*

Richard Castellano (September 4, 1933 — December 10, 1988)

Castellano was nominated for an Oscar for his role in *Lovers and Other Strangers*. He played Peter Clemenza in *The Godfather*.

Ed Wood (October 10, 1924 — December 10, 1978)

Director Ed Wood, famous for the movies *Glen or Glenda?* and *Plan 9 From Outer Space*, won the Golden Turkey Award for Worst Director of All Time. Now a cult favorite, he was the subject of a Tim Burton biopic, *Ed Wood*, starring Johnny Depp, which won two Oscars.

Business

Armand Hammer (May 21, 1898 — December 10, 1990)

Business tycoon Armand Hammer ran Occidental Petroleum, and was also well known for his art collection, philanthropy, and his business and diplomatic work with the Soviet Union. He is the subject of five biographies and two autobiographies.

Poster for the Ed Wood film *Plan 9 From Outer Space*.

Horace Dodge (May 17, 1868 — December 10, 1920)

American automobile manufacturing pioneer Horace Elgin Dodge co-founded the Dodge Brothers Company. Originally a supplier to Oldsmobile and Ford, Dodge began producing cars in 1917. Ford bought Dodge in 1919, and sold the brand to Chrysler in 1928.

Musicians

Rick Danko (December 29, 1942 — December 10, 1999)

Canadian musician and singer, Rick Danko is most famous as a member of The Band. As part of that group, he was elected to the Rock and Roll Hall of Fame in 1994.

FARON YOUNG

Faron Young (February 25, 1932 — December 10, 1996)

Honky-tonk country star Faron Young (left), known as the "Hillbilly Heartthrob," committed suicide in 1996. He is a member of the Country Music Hall of Fame.

Jascha Heifetz (February 2 [O.S. January 20], 1901 — December 10, 1987)

Jascha Heifetz is considered one of the greatest violinists of all time. Born in Lithuania, then part of the Russian Empire, Heifetz was recognized as a child prodigy, making his public debut at the age of 7. He and his family left Russia for the United States in 1917, and he had a long and distinguished career as a performer and recording artist. (For an explanation of "O.S.," see "On Dates" on page 56.)

Otis Redding (September 9, 1941 — December 10, 1967)

A major figure in soul and R&B music, Otis Redding was known as the "King of Soul," Redding's biggest hit is "(Sittin' On) The Dock of the Bay," released in 1968 following Redding's death in a plane crash.

Otis Redding

Politics and Government

Augusto Pinochet (November 25, 1915 — December 10, 2006)

Chilean General Augusto Pinochet led a coup d'état in 1973 and established a military dictatorship that ruled Chile from 1973 to 1990.

Eugene McCarthy (March 29, 1916 — December 10, 2006)

Eugene McCarthy, Democratic senator from Minnesota, challenged incumbent Lyndon Johnson for the Democratic presidential nomination in 1968, running on an anti-Vietnam War platform. His delegate victory in New Hampshire led to Johnson's decision to withdraw from the race.

Franjo Tuđman (May 14, 1922 — December 10, 1999)

A Croatian politician, Tuđman was the first President of Croatia following its separation from Yugoslavia.

Red Cloud (1822? — December 10, 1909)

A war leader and chief of the Oglala Lakota (Sioux), Red Cloud (Lakota: *Maȟpíya Lúta*) was known as one of the most capable Native American opponents of the US Army. His campaign, Red Cloud's War (1866-1868), led to the Treaty of Fort Laramie.

Red Cloud (right) with Oglala chief American Horse (left).
Photo Credit: John C. H. Grabill

Religion and Philosophy

Thomas Merton (January 31, 1915 — December 10, 1968)

American Trappist monk Thomas Merton wrote more than 70 books on spirituality, social justice, and pacifism, as well as poetry. His best-selling autobiography, *The Seven Storey Mountain* (1948), inspired numerous youth to enter the Catholic priesthood and monastic orders.

Karl Barth (May 10, 1886 — December 10, 1968)

Swiss Reformed theologian Karl Barth (left) was described by Pope Pius XII as "the most important theologian since Thomas Aquinas." His approach, known as dialectical theology, is also known as neo-orthodoxy.

Averroes (April 14, 1126 — December 10, 1198)

Averroes, also known as Ibn Rushd (ابن رشد), who lived in what became Spain and Morocco, developed a school of philosophy known as Averroism, reconciling Aristotelian ideas with the Islamic faith. He was hugely controversial in both the Christian and Islamic worlds.

Science and Education

Sir Joseph Dalton Hooker (June 30, 1817 — December 10, 1911)

Botanist and explorer Sir Joseph Dalton Hooker was Director of the Royal Botanical Gardens in Kew. An early figure in the acceptance of the Theory of Evolution, Hooker became a close friend of Charles Darwin and was part of the famous Oxford Debates on the topic.

Sir Joseph Dalton Hooker

Alfred Nobel (October 21, 1833 — December 10, 1896)

Chemist, engineer, and armaments manufacturer Alfred Nobel (left, painting by Emil Österman) held over 350 patents, most famously for dynamite. Best known for using his fortune to create the Nobel Prizes, the synthetic element nobelium was named for him. The Nobel Prizes are awarded each year on the anniversary of his death.

Sports

Adolph Rupp (September 2, 1901 — December 10, 1977)

One of the most successful coaches in the history of American college basketball, Adolph Rupp coached the Kentucky Wildcats from 1930 to 1972. He was elected to the Basketball Hall of Fame in 1969.

Walter Johnson (November 6, 1887 — December 10, 1946)

Walter Johnson (left), known as "Barney" and "The Big Train" was an MLB pitcher who spent 21 years with the Washington Senators, later managing the Senators and the Cleveland Indians. He holds numerous pitching records, and was the first player to achieve more than 3,000 strikeouts.

Baseball card of Walter Johnson

Words

Algernon Blackwood (March 14, 1869 — December 10, 1951)

English author Algernon Blackwood (right, sketch by "14nu5") is famous as one of the most prolific authors of ghost stories and tales of the supernatural.

Damon Runyon (October 4, 1880 — December 10, 1946)

Newspaperman and author Damon Runyon is famous for his stories about the world of Broadway during Prohibition. His stories formed the basis of the musical *Guys and Dolls*.

Luigi Pirandello (June 28, 1867 — December 10, 1936)

Italian writer Luigi Pirandello won the Nobel Prize in Literature in 1934. He is considered a forerunner of the Theatre of the Absurd.

December
The Twelfth Month

"In cold December fragrant chaplets blow,
And heavy harvests nod beneath the snow."

— Alexander Pope, *Dunciad*.

In Latin, *decem* means "ten," so it may seem strange that December is actually the twelfth month of the year. The original Roman calendar, from which our month names come, began in March, making December indeed the tenth month.

No one is completely sure when the start of the year was moved to January, but the traditional name of December stuck.

In the northern hemisphere, December is the month with the shortest daylight hours of the year; in the southern hemisphere, it's the opposite. December is the equivalent of June in the southern hemisphere, and vice versa.

In the Julian and Gregorian calendars, December is the twelfth and last month of the year, and is one of seven months with 31 days.

In every year, December starts on the same day of the week as September, and ends on the same day of the week as April.

The length of the day varies through the year, because the Earth tilts as it revolves around the Sun. The two extremes are known as the *solstices*, and the points at which day and night are of equal length are known as the *equinoxes*. The northern hemisphere's winter solstice, which is the shortest day of the year, falls in December. In the southern hemisphere, the summer solstice, the longest day of the year, falls in December.

The dates of the solstice can vary between December 20 and 22. Because even the ancients could tell when the days stopped getting shorter (or longer) and started in the other direction, many holidays and festivals take place around the time of the solstice, including most famously Christmas.

December in Other Cultures

In Albanian, the month of December is known as *Dhjetor*. In Egyptian Arabic, it's ديسمبر (pronounced *dīsambar*). In Czech, it's *Prosinec*, in Finland it's *Joulukuu*, and in Poland it's *Grudzień*. Hungarians say *Karácsony hava*.

In Greek, the month of Δεκέμβριος is pronounced *Dekémbrios*. In Hebrew, it's דצמבר and Hindi, it's दिसंबर.

In Irish Gaelic, the month of December is *Nollaig mi na Nollag* and in Scottish Gaelic it's *an Dùbhlachd*. The Welsh say *Rhagfyr*.

The Chinese and Japanese both write the month 十二月, but it is pronounced differently in

Cantonese, Mandarin, and Japanese. Koreans write it as 십이월, or *Sipiweol*. In Vietnam it's 腊月𬺿 *(Tháng mười hai)*.

In Old English, the month is *Gēolmōnaþ* and in Anglo-Saxon it's *Ærra-ġēola mōnaþ*.

The month of December does not correspond exactly with months in other calendar systems. The Hebrew months of כִּסְלֵו (*Kislev*) and טֵבֵת (*Tevet*) overlap December, as do the Persian months of آذر (*Azar*) and دی (*Dey*) and the Hindu months of मार्गशीर्ष (*Mārgaśirṣa*) and पूस (*Pauṣa*).

In the Islamic world, the lunar calendar consists of 354 or 355 days, meaning that the months slowly migrate through the year, and over time different months correspond to December.

December Superstitions

- "A green December fills the graveyard."
- "When December snows fall fast, marry and true love will last."
- "A December bride will be fond of novelty, entertaining but extravagant."

December Symbols

Birthstone: December birthstones in various traditions include turquoise, lapiz lazuli, zircon, blue topaz, and tanzanite.

Oil painting on lapis lazuli, *Perseus Rescuing Andromeda*, by Giuseppe Cesari.

Birth Flowers: December's flowers are the narcissus and the holly.

Illustration by Anton Hartinger from *Atlas der Alpenflora* (1882)

December Events

Honorary Months

Presidents, Congresses, and nations around the world issue proclamations recognizing particular months to honor certain causes. Other organizations, less formal in nature, do the same thing. These events generally fall in December. (All US unless noted otherwise.)

- Bingo's Birthday Month (the game, not the dog)
- Food Service Safety Month (Worldwide)
- National Critical Infrastructure Protection Month
- National Egg Nog Month
- National Fruit Cake Month
- National Impaired Driving Prevention Month
- National Sign Up for Summer Camp Month
- National Stress-Free Family Holiday Month
- Safe Toys and Gifts Month
- Spiritual Literacy Month
- Write a Business Plan Month

Moveable and Multi-Day Events

Some events take place over a specific week or time period. Start and finish dates may vary from year to year. Some events occur on different days each year (such as "fourth Saturday of a month").

Advent (Christianity)
The four weeks prior to Christmas are known as the Advent season, a time of expectant waiting and preparation for the celebration of the Nativity of Jesus.

Hanukkah (חֲנֻכָּה) (Judaism)
The Jewish celebration of Hanukkah, also known as the Festival of Lights or the Feast of Dedication, takes place for eight days and nights beginning on the 25th day of Kislev, which varies from late November to late December. It commemorates the rededication of the Second Temple in Jerusalem at the time of the Maccabean Revolt.

Each night of Hanukkah is marked by lighting one branch of the Menorah, a candelabrum with nine branches. In addition to prayers, celebrants eat foods fried or baked in olive oil. Children play with a spinning top known as a dreidel and receive Hanukkah gelt.

18th century painting of a Hanukkah celebration, artist unknown.

Karthikai Deepam (கார்த்திகை விளக்கீடு) (Hindu Tamil)

The Hindu Tamil celebration of Karthikai Deepam takes place in mid-November to mid-December when the moon is in conjunction with the Pleiades (*Karthigai*). It is a religious festival of lamps and also celebrates the bonding between brothers and sisters.

Lager Beer Week (Secular)

The second week in December is dedicated to lager beer.

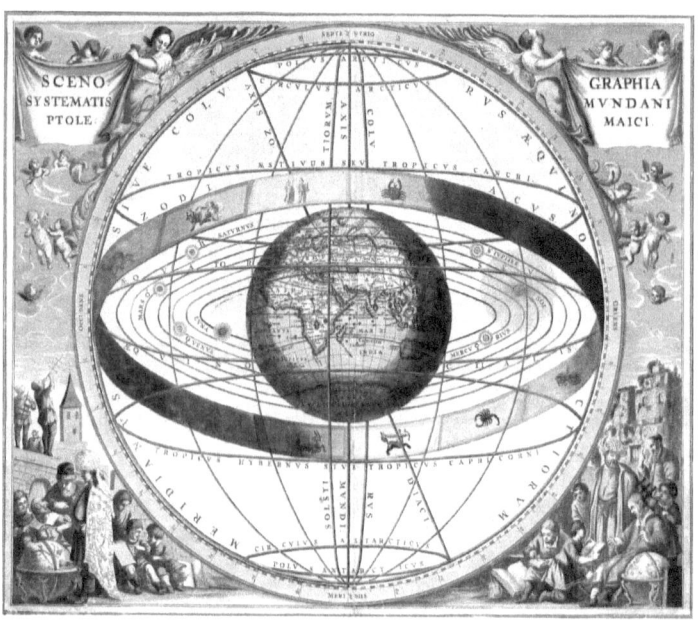

The signs of the zodiac in the Ptolemaic view of the university, by
Johannes van Loon (1660)

December 10 Zodiac Signs

From the perspective of someone on Earth, the Sun appears to move through the sky throughout the year, along a path astronomers call the ecliptic plane. The ecliptic plane is divided into twelve constellations, known as the zodiac, based on traditionally observed patterns of stars. On your birthday, you can't see your constellation, because it's part of the daytime sky.

The zodiac was first developed by Babylonian astronomers about 2,500 years ago. Because they were unaware that the Earth wobbles like a spinning top (a motion known as *precession*), they didn't make allowance for the fact that the Sun's path through the zodiac changes over time.

That means there are now two sets of dates for your birth sign. The *tropical* dates are the original Babylonian dates; the *sidereal* dates tell you where the Sun actually appears as it moves along its annual path.

In tropical reckoning, December 10 is in Sagittarius, and in siderial reckoning, December 10 is in Scorpio.

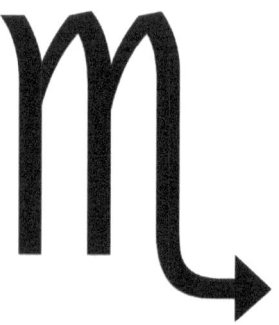

Scorpio

Tropical *October 23 to November 21*

Sidereal *November 16 to December 15*

Scorpio, the Scorpion, appears in the Greek myth of the hunter Orion. Because Orion had touched the robes of the goddess Artemis, in revenge, the goddess had the scorpion kill Orion. As a reward, she placed the scorpion in the sky, where it chases Orion through the eternal night.

The constellation of Scorpius includes the red giant star Antares, which is so large that the entire Solar System through the orbit of Mars would be inside it.

Scorpio is a fire sign, and people born under this sign are supposed to be determined, reserved, loyal, and secretive. Scorpios are supposed to be compatible with the water signs of Pisces and Capricorn.

Sagittarius

Tropical: *November 23 to December 21*
Sidereal: *December 16 to January 14*

Sagittarius means "archer" in Latin. The constellation in the night sky is often depicted as having the appearance of a stick-figure archer drawing its bow.

The brighter stars in Sagittarius form an asterism known as The Teapot. The Milky Way is densest in Sagittarius, because the galactic center lies in that direction.

In astrology, Sagittarius is a fire sign. People born under it are said to be not superstitious. They are supposed to be drawn toward travel and philosophy, and to enjoy social contacts, meeting new people, and exploring other cultures. They are also said to be highly intelligent, visionary, and tolerant.

Sagittarians are considered compatible with Aries, Leo, and Gemini, and to a lesser extent with Taurus and Virgo.

Illustration by Edward Penfield

What Day of the Week is December 10?

On what day of the week does December 10 fall?

Surprisingly, this isn't an easy question. Because the calendar year is 365 days long (366 in leap years), it doesn't divide evenly by the seven days of the week.

Also, the Earth goes around the Sun in about 365-1/4 days, so a calendar tends to drift over time. That's why the same date falls on different weekdays in different years.

This is made even more complicated by a change in calendars that took place in 1582. Our modern calendar has its roots in ancient Rome, in a calendar reform conducted by Julius Caesar. Caesar commissioned mathematicians to attack the problem, and they came up with the idea of *leap years,* and thus standardized the calendar for centuries to come. This was called the *Julian calendar.*

Over time, however, the small errors in Caesar's calculation compounded. That's why Pope Gregory XIII commissioned the *Gregorian calendar,* used in most of the world today. Some countries converted in 1582, when the calendar was first developed;

some converted later; other still haven't changed.

Gregorian and Julian aren't the only types of calendars. The Hebrew year, the Islamic year, and many other calendars are used in different parts of the world and among different people.

You can convert Gregorian dates to other calendars, including the Hebrew calendar, the Islamic calendar, and even the Mayan calendar by visiting the Fourmilab Calendar Converter at http://www.fourmilab.ch/documents/calendar/.

Chinese calendar systems are quite complex and have changed several times; a full discussion is far beyond the scope of this book. If you're interested, you can find information here: http://www.hermetic.ch/cal_stud/chinese_cal.htm.

A 50-year brass perpetual calendar.

Copyright, Credit, and Contact

Follow Us

Our blog *Dobson's Improbable History* (http://improbhistory.blogspot.com) features short articles on events and people associated with each day, and updates several times each week. You can also get a daily "What Happened In History" message and all the latest Timespinner Press news by following us on Facebook at https://www.facebook.com/TimespinnerPress. Our Twitter feed @SidewiseThinker links you to all our News of the Day.

Contact Us

Find an error or a format problem? Want information about the series, about us, or about when the volume for your special day might be available? Please email us at editor@timespinnerpress.com. (We also take requests if your special day isn't yet complete. Please give us at least six weeks' notice if possible.)

On Dates

Historians use "CE" (Common Era) and "BCE" (Before the Common Era) instead of the more common "AD" (*Anno Domini*, or Year of Our Lord) and "BC" (Before Christ), reflecting the fact that the year-numbering system established by the Gregorian calendar is used throughout the world in many countries not culturally Christian.

The CE/BCE designation dates back to at least 1708, and has been adopted as a standard by the United Nations and the Universal Postal Union. Because this series of books covers events and people of all nations and cultures, we use the CE/BCE terms.

The abbreviation "O.S." ("Old Style") on some dates refers to the fact that the Russian Empire did not switch from the Julian to the Gregorian calendar at the same time as the rest of Europe, and therefore some figures and events have two dates. (See "What Day of the Week…" for an explanation of Julian and Gregorian dates.)

People and events whose original names are not in the Western alphabet have their native names (where possible) in the appropriate script shown in parenthesis. If you are using an e-reader to access an electronic version of this book, all characters don't always display on all devices.

Sources and Art Credits

We owe a great debt to Wikipedia, which is our first stop for research. We attempt to make independent confirmation of all important dates and facts through a variety of other sources. Other sources we frequently use include the Library of Congress; "on this day" listings from *Encyclopedia Britannica*, the New York *Times*, and the BBC; and, of course, the always essential Google.

All art and photographs are either in the public domain, used under a Creative Commons license, or with a "fair use" justification, and most frequently come from Wikimedia Commons and the Library of Congress Prints and Photographs Division.

Attribution is provided where requested by the copyright owner or when of historical significance, listed below. For information about any particular illustration or photograph, please contact us.

- The photograph of Edward, Prince of Wales during his 1919 Canada trip used on the cover is in the public domain because its copyright has expired.

- The 1936 portrait photograph of Wallis Simpson used on the cover was published in *The Sketch*, and is in the public domain because the photographer is unknown and the photograph is more than 70 years old.

- The vector image of the Coat of Arms of the Duke of Windsor used on the cover and in the "Event of the Day" article was created by "Sodacan" and is used here under CC-BY-SA 3.0. The coat of arms itself is not an object of copyright.

- The scanned copy of the Instrument of Abdication of King Edward VIII used on the cover is in the public domain.

- The illustration of the month of December used on the back cover and as the frontispiece is from the 15th century French Gothic illuminated manuscript *Les Très Riches Heures du duc de Berry* by the Limbourg Brothers, Jean Colombe, and an intermediate painter whose name is lost to history. It is in the public domain because its copyright has expired.

- The photograph of King Edward VIII and Wallis Simpson during their 1936 Mediterranean cruise is from the *Daily Herald* archive at the British National Media Museum. The Museum states that no known copyright restrictions exist on the use of this image.

- The painting *Portrait of Catherine Howard* by Hans Holbein the Younger was created between 1540 and 1540, and is in the public domain because its copyright has expired. Versions of this painting exist in London's National Portrait Gallery and in the Toledo (Ohio) Museum of Art. Recent research suggests that the painting is not actually of Catherine Howard, but rather of an unknown woman, possibly a member of the Cromwell family. The painting is credited both to Hans Holbein the Younger and "after Hans Holbein the Younger," suggesting a copy or derivative work, possibly one created by someone working in Holbein's studio.

- The portrait photograph of Alfred Nobel was taken by Gösta Florman prior to 1896 and is in the public domain because its copyright has expired.

- The official Nobel Prize photograph of Theodore Roosevelt, taken in 1906, is in the public domain because its copyright has expired.

- The 1912 promotional poster for the *Vin Fiz* coast-to-coast flight is in the public domain because its copyright has expired.

- The still frame of Mighty Mouse from the 1945 animated cartoon "Wolf! Wolf!" is in the public domain because its copyright has expired. The character and image of Mighty Mouse are trademarked by CBS Operations, and no challenge to such trademark status is intended or implied.

- The 1968 photograph of Dan Blocker as Hoss Cartwright from the TV series *Bonanza* is in the public domain because it was published in the United States between 1923 and 1977 without a copyright notice.

- The 1938 photograph of Dorothy Lamour on the cover of the Argentinian magazine *Cinelandia* is the in public domain because its copyright in its home country has expired.

- The cropped trailer screenshot of Una Merkel from the 1935 film *Baby Face Harrington* is in the public domain because it was published in the United States between 1923 and 1977 without a copyright notice.

- The 1966 publicity photograph of Chad & Jeremy from a CBS Television special is in the public domain because it was published in the United States between 1923 and 1977 without a copyright notice.

- The 1966 publicity photograph of Chet Huntley and David Brinkley from *The Huntley-Brinkley Report* is in the public domain because it was published in the United States between 1923 and 1977 without a copyright notice.

- The 1836 portrait of Ada Lovelace was painted by Margaret Sarah Carpenter, and is in the public domain because its copyright has expired. The original is in the British Government Art Collection at 10 Downing Street in London.

- The 1848 daguerreotype of Emily Dickinson is part of the Todd-Bingham Picture Collection at Yale University. It is in the public domain because its copyright has expired. This version has been cropped and cleaned up to remove scratches and other imperfections.

- The 1863 portrait photograph of George MacDonald was taken by *Alice in Wonderland* author Lewis Carroll (Rev. Charles Dodgson). It is in the public domain because its copyright has expired.

- The 1973 publicity photo of Richard Pryor from the CBS Television special *Lily* is in the public domain because it was published in the United States between 1923 and 1977 without a copyright notice. It has been cropped for its use here.

- The 1959 film poster from *Plan 9 from Outer Space* is in the public domain because it was published in the United States between 1923 and 1977 without a copyright notice. While there may or may not have been an original copyright, such copyright (if any) was not renewed.

- The Capitol Records promotional photograph of Faron Young is in the public domain because it was published in the United States between 1923 and 1977 without a copyright notice.

- The 1967 Volt Records promotional photograph of Otis Redding originally appeared in *Billboard* magazine. It is in the public domain because it was published in the United States between 1923 and 1977 without a copyright notice.

- The 1891 photograph of Red Cloud and American Horse was taken by John C. H. Grabill and is part of the Grabill Collection at the Library of Congress. It is in the public domain because its copyright has expired.

- The 1955 photograph of Karl Barth was taken by Maria Netter. It is used here under CC-BY-SA 3.0.

- The photograph of Sir Joseph Dalton Hooker is in the public domain because its copyright has expired. The photographer is unknown.

- The painting of Alfred Nobel is by Emil Österman. It is in the public domain because its copyright has expired.

- The 1909-1911 American Tobacco baseball card of Walter Johnson is in the public domain because its copyright has expired.

- The pen sketch of Algernon Blackwood is by "14nu5" and is used here under CC-BY-SA 3.0.

- The 16th century oil on lapis lazuli painting of *Perseus Rescuing Andromeda* is by Giuseppe Cesari. It is in the public domain because its copyright has expired. The original object is in the collection of the Saint Louis Art Museum.

- The 1882 painting of *Ilex aquifolium* (holly) is by Anton Hartinger, and appeared originally in the book Atlas der Alpenflora.

- The artist who created the 18th century painting of a Hannukah celebration is unknown. The painting is in the public domain because its copyright has expired.

- The 1660 drawing of the heavens is by Johannes van Loon, and was first published in *Harmonia Macrocosmica* by Andreas Cellarius. It is in the public domain because its copyright has expired.

- The photograph of the 1906 automobile calendar by
  Edward Penfield is from the Library of Congress Prints
  and Photographs Division, and is in the public domain
  because it was published prior to January 1, 1923.

- The 50-year perpetual calendar photograph is in the
  public domain.

- The painting on the last page, *Labors of the Month:
  December*, by Simon Bening, was published in a Flemish
  Book of Hours in the first half of the 16th century. It is
  in the public domain because its copyright has expired.

License Description and Terms

Aside from material purely in the public domain,
photographs and other material in this book are used
under specific licenses permitting free use, usually
with attribution. For full text and terms of these
licenses, click or enter the appropriate links below.

- Creative Commons Attribution 2.0 Generic (CC-BY
  2.0): http://creativecommons.org/licenses/by/2.0/
  deed.en

- Creative Commons Attribution-Share Alike 3.0 Generic
  (CC-BY-SA 3.0): http://creativecommons.org/
  licenses/by-sa/3.0/

- Creative Commons Attribution-Share Alike 2.5 Generic
  (CC-BY-SA 2.5): http://creativecommons.org/
  licenses/by-sa/2.5/deed.en

- Creative Commons Attribution-Share Alike 2.0 Generic
  (CC-BY-SA 2.0): http://creativecommons.org/
  licenses/by/2.0/deed.en http://
  creativecommons.org/publicdomain/zero/1.0/
  deed.en

Timespinner
Press

Labors of the Month: December, by Simon Bening